THE PHANTOM
STRUGGLE

THE PHANTOM
STRUGGLE

Memoirs of A Life Once Struggling

OMAR GONZALEZ

Rise Above Publishing LLC
Kansas City, MO

THE PHANTOM STRUGGLE:
MEMOIRS OF A LIFE ONCE STRUGGLING
Copyright © 2020 by Omar Gonzalez

Cover design by Youness El Hindami

First Rise Above Publishing edition - August 2020

Print Book ISBN: 978-1-7356242-0-4
Ebook ISBN: 978-1-7356242-1-1

Library of Congress Control Number: 2020915721

Rise Above Publishing LLC
Kansas City, MO

*For those of you struggling
to keep your struggles
unknown to the world*

CONTENTS

INTRODUCTION   3

CHAPTER 1   9
  Some

CHAPTER 2   15
  Knives, Tears, & Tuna-fish Sandwiches

CHAPTER 3   21
  Gonzalez

CHAPTER 4   27
  Sunny on A Cloudy Day

CHAPTER 5   43
  Skipping School

CHAPTER 6   49
  Over & Over

CHAPTER 7   55
  Never Out

CHAPTER 8   63
  Lust vs Love

CHAPTER 9   69
  The Endless Climb

CHAPTER 10   73
  Lately

CHAPTER 11   79
  We Three

EPILOGUE   83

"More than 10 percent of U.S. children live with a parent with alcohol problems."

For more information, please visit:
https://www.niaaa.nih.gov

"On average, nearly 20 people per minute are physically abused by an intimate partner in the United States. During one year, this equates to more than 10 million women and men."

"1 in 15 children are exposed to intimate partner violence each year, and 90% of these children are eyewitnesses to this violence."

For more information, please visit:
https://www.ncadv.org

If you or anyone you believe may need help, please call The National Domestic Violence Hotline
1-800-799 SAFE (7233)

Or go online to
https://www.DomesticShelters.org

THE PHANTOM
STRUGGLE

INTRODUCTION

"I can honestly say that there is really nothing about myself that puzzles me these days. I am content with who I am and how it is that I came to be this way. I am a hard-working individual with an impervious will to achieve whatever I set my mind to. I have always been this way for as long as I can remember. For me, to be puzzled by an aspect of myself is the same as admitting that I am discontent with myself. Since such perplexity is absent within me, I will instead piece together my life experiences with psychological perspectives in order to provide a broader sense as to who I am and why I rarely wonder about the way I am. Although psychology provides seven perspectives to try to explain and understand an individual's behavior and mental processes, I have chosen the three that make the most sense out of my life; Behavior Genetics, Psychodynamic, and Behavioral.

So, am I a product of the kind of behaviors I observed during my upbringing (Behavioral), are my character traits due to shortcomings or traumas I experienced in my life (Psychodynamic), or am I just the result of genetic endowment (Behavior Genetics)? When delving deep into my past and reminiscing over the experiences that stand out the most in my life, the answer is quite simple: I am the product of all three perspectives. Albeit, more so the genetic perspective in my opinion, but the other perspectives did serve their purpose. Anyhow, I am the product of a turbulent, alcohol-ridden, and low-income home. During my first nine years that my father was around, I witnessed verbal and physical marital abuse quite often. I experienced intense loathing and unfair discipline from my mother. The relationship between my brother and me was tumultuous for most of our childhood. My mother, brother, and I also spent a few years moving around from different homes. My late childhood years through my late adolescent years were spent in a church environment. Contrarily, my experiences there were also a bit volatile. Clearly, one can deduce that it was through these experiences that the Behavioral and Psychodynamic perspectives originated in my life. Even though the struggles I faced at times may have seemed too overwhelming, I endured.

I endured because I believe it was in my nature to endure and adapt to whatever type of environment, I ever found myself in. This is where the Behavior Genetics perspective comes into play. It would not be wrong to assume that my parents were monsters, but that was not always the case. When not chugging down an entire bottle of alcohol, they were actually good people. They were both hard workers, humble, and family-centered people. I know I inherited all of their positive traits. I can see it when looking back at all that I have overcome and achieved in my life. A feeling inside my gut, heart, and mind constantly accompanied me through my many ventures. It would be a lie for me to say that I had somewhat of a role model that I looked upon. Honestly, all I can say is that I followed my feelings. If the situations and external factors I came across served a vital role in my life, it was simply to reveal and further strengthen the indomitable will I possessed.

Overall, it can be surmised that my character has been hardened throughout most of my life. Given all the obstacles I had to overcome, I didn't have the luxury of taking it easy, quitting, or coming to terms with my weaknesses. Had I given in to such a mentality, it is most likely that I would not have made it this far. I am not stating that my life is or should be the standard of how to produce a responsible or strong-minded person. Like everyone, I am not perfect. I have had my fair share of flaws that I have had to learn to improve. However, it is the overcoming part that I embrace the most in my life. Whether it was overcoming homelessness or going to sleep on an empty stomach, prevailing over such circumstances is what made me realize I was resilient and adaptable. Today, as a grown man who has been on his own for quite some time, I am able to balance school, work, household chores, and many other responsibilities. I am not some child inside of a man's body still trying to find or understand himself; I found myself a long time ago. I know and understand who I am, what my goals are, and what I am capable of".

— My first assignment for Dr. Nancy King's psychology class.

CHAPTER 1

SOME

Lights,

Revealing,

Some blinding.

Wise men,

Honest,

Some deceitful.

Addictions,

Life-threatening,

Some life-saving.

Facts,

Useful,

Some wasteful.

Treasures,

Precious,

Some worthless.

Truths,

Healing,

Some damaging.

Lives,

Finite,

Some Everlasting.

CHAPTER 2

KNIVES,
TEARS,
&
TUNA-FISH
SANDWICHES

"Please stop, Mom. You're acting like a nut!" yell two young boys. Dismissing their pleas, the mother raises a knife to her neck. As she is about to cut, the boys muster up enough strength to yell even louder, "Why Mom? Why are you doing this?" Suddenly, she pauses and sits there motionless, holding the knife ever so steady. Beginning to cry, she looks at her two sons and says, "I hurt so bad. I just want it all to end already!" Feeling their mother's distress, the boys frantically begin apologizing for anything they may have done to cause her to want to cut her own skin. Amidst the chaos, she reaches out to one of her sons and asks, "But don't you hate me?" Then, reaching out to her other son, she asks, "Don't you both hate me?" "No Mom! We don't hate you! We love you Mom!" yell the boys, desperately trying to save her.

Continuing to plead with her, they say, "We hate him, mom. We hate that monster! We hate it when he hurts you! We hate it when he hurts us! We need you, Mom!" Becoming unafraid of the knife in her hands, the boys embrace their mother so hard and begin to cry with her. "When we grow big and strong, we'll put a beating on him Mom," promises one of the boys as the three continue to cry together. After a few minutes, all the crying stops, and the three of them release their embrace from each other. A moment of silence engulfs the room as the mother looks down at the knife in her hand. As she begins to walk away from the boys, she asks, "Would you guys like some tuna fish sandwiches?"

CHAPTER 3

GONZALEZ

The Name,

Passed down to me at birth.

The Demons,

Synonymous with the name.

The bane,

Although undesired, I never had a choice.

The fight,

Remains unrelenting and ever strong.

The pain,

However, begins to settle within,

The veins.

And so, it becomes harder to fight.

The body,

Will it ever cease to move?

The mind,

Will it ever give in?

The answer,

I must refuse such thoughts.

The truth,

I was meant to break the chain.

The legend,

I was the Gonzalez,

Who rose above!

CHAPTER 4

SUNNY
ON
A
CLOUDY
DAY

There are dark days,

In life, that just may,

Seem to cloudy for,

Any light to break through,

And help people to see.

There are dark moments in life,

Where the suffering that,

Occurred is just to painful,

For people to forget or,

Even talk about.

Although she knows this,

She just can't wait any longer.

She knows that she has to,

Bring her sons out into the,

Open, and pour her heart,

Out to them.

Although She believes that,

She has only one shot to,

Finally make amends with,

Her sons, she takes a deep,

Breath, looks up and gazes,

For a moment, as if trying to,

Gain strength from a sun,

That just isn't there.

And so, she begins to say,

"Oh, my dear sons, there's,

Nothing more that I want,

Than to hold you both as,

Tight as I can, just so that,

You could feel how sorry I am.

But I know that is not enough,

Especially not for you,

My baby boy.

I know that my words, right now,

May not reach deep enough to,

Push aside and replace the,

Horrid things I used to say or do,

To you, especially to you,

My baby boy.

Please believe me when I say,

That I'd do anything to undo,

The past. I'd even go back to,

One of the times, when I was in,

So deep, and just swim down,

If it meant you'd grow up to be,

Much happier than you are now,

Without me. Especially you,

My baby boy.

But as hard as I wish for that,

I know that just isn't possible.

But I know with all of my heart,

That all is not lost between us,

My sons, especially between you,

And me, my baby boy.

I know this because I look back,

To where we started, and the fact,

We're alive is nothing more than,

A miracle. We've made it to this,

Point in life together. That has,

To stand for something."

Upon saying her piece,

A great silence befalls,

The three of them. And so,

Not knowing what to do,

But also, not wanting to,

Disturb this brief moment of,

Peace, she simply stands still,

As tears fall from her eyes.

Feeling lost and weary, she,

Becomes startled by an,

Unexpected grab of her hand.

Her oldest son has heard her,

Piece and has made peace with it.

He wraps his arms around her,

And holds her as tight as he can,

And says, "I forgive you mom,

And I love you."

Although this brings her great joy,

She knows that all is still not right,

As her baby boy has yet to speak,

And say his piece or make peace,

With her.

Standing a few feet from her and,

The oldest, he simply stands there,

Looking toward the calm river.

Suddenly, her baby boy begins,

To walk slowly toward the river.

Not knowing what to do,

But also, not wanting to,

Disturb this brief moment of,

Peace, she and the oldest,

Simply follow behind him.

Nearing the edge, he comes to a,

Stop, and so she and her oldest,

Also stop just a few feet behind.

She patiently waits for her baby boy,

But knows all too well that his piece,

For her is full of unimaginable pain,

And that making peace with her may,

Very well be the most difficult thing,

He's done or will ever do.

Suddenly, she notices him take a deep,

Breath, look up and gaze for a moment,

As if trying to gain strength from a sun,

That just isn't there.

And so, he begins to say,

"I never asked to be a part of the game,

You and Pops were playing with us.

I never wanted to be able to take as,

Much pain as I am able to take.

I never wished to be able to hold back,

All of the tears that I've held back.

I never hoped that I'd become his,

Favorite son. But you guys never,

Really gave me much of a choice,

Did you?"

Taking a pause from saying his piece,

His lips begin to quiver and she,

Takes notice. Wanting to comfort him,

She moves toward him but he steps,

Back fast and sternly says, "No".

Not knowing what to do,

But also, not wanting to push,

Her baby boy farther than he,

Already is, she simply stands still,

And watches as he takes a deep,

Breath, looks up and gazes for a moment,

As if trying to gain strength from a sun,

That just isn't there.

As tears fall from his eyes,

He continues, "I only did what I thought,

Was best to do to avoid more pain.

I used to fucking hate Pops so much!

Watching Pops hurt you and my brother,

The way he did and being powerless,

To stop him but at last, I thought I had it,

Figured out. I'd make myself strong,

Enough to take the worst Pops had to,

Dish out. I hoped that I'd take it all,

And that he'd become so tired that,

He had nothing left to take out on,

You guys. How was I suppose to,

Know just how twisted Pops was,

That he'd come to admire just how,

Much pain I could take and claim,

Me as his favorite son?

But despite that, I still hated him,

And wanted nothing more than to,

One day be strong enough to put,

A great hurting on him.

But then the day came when you,

Betrayed me.

The day came when you left me,

All alone.

The day came when you protected,

Only him from Pops.

The day came when you started to,

Beat me so hard, just to see if you,

Could get the tears out of me.

There were days when you wouldn't,

Even smile once at me.

And what's even more shocking,

There were days when you inflicted,

More and worse pain on me than,

Even Pops did!"

Taking a pause from saying his piece,

His body begins to quiver,

And he struggles trying to regain,

His composure.

She and his older brother want,

Nothing more than to reach out,

And hold him as tight as they can,

Just to let him know that he is no,

Longer alone and that it is safe,

For him to let go of all the pain he,

Has been holding back.

Not knowing what to do,

But also, not wanting to push,

Him farther than he already is,

They simply stand still and watch,

As he takes a deep breath, looks up,

And gazes for a moment, as if trying,

To gain strength from the sliver of,

Light breaking through the dark,

And cloudy sky.

Still crying, he struggles to continue,

But manages to say, "I'm sorry mom.

I'm sorry bro. I'm so sorry! I'm sorry,

For being able to take as much pain,

As I can. I'm sorry for being able to,

Hold back as much tears as I have.

I'm sorry for becoming his favorite son.

I'm sorry for anything I might've,

Done to cause you to hate me.

I'm sorry mom, for whatever I did to,

Cause you to want to hurt me.

I only did what I thought was best,

To protect you both."

Succumbing to the pain and,

Becoming weary from the waterfall,

Of tears he is finally letting go of,

Her baby boy falls to his knees.

Knowing what to do, so that he,

Doesn't fall further than he has,

She and his older brother kneel,

Beside him, reach out, and begin,

To hold him as tight as they can.

Although she knows that nothing,

Can be done to push aside or erase,

All of the horrid things her baby boy,

Has experienced, she remains hopeful,

That having finally said his piece,

Her baby boy can finally have peace.

A few minutes have passed by as,

The three of them are now just sitting,

On the grass in peaceful silence.

Suddenly, something grabs their attention.

Standing up, the three of them look up,

And simply watch. They take a deep breath,

And gaze a little longer, as if trying,

To gain strength from the bright,

Light of the sun that now illuminates,

Their path home.

CHAPTER 5

SKIPPING SCHOOL

"Let's ride to Boulevard East."

Go, Go, Go!

"Let's take the long way."

Go, Turn, Go!

"Yo, but there's mad 5-0 that way."

Go, Go, Go!

"Then what way asshole?"

Go, Turn, Go!

"Hey, who you calling asshole, fuckface?"

Go, Go, Go!

"Relax guys, let's just cut through West New

York."

Go, Turn, Go!

"Watch the immi bus!"

Go, Go, Go!

"Diablo! Mother fucker came out of nowhere!"

Go, Turn, Go!

"It's a god damn immi bus, you blind fuck!"

Go, Go, Go!

"Yo, but how bout you hop off my—."

Stop!

"Holy shit! You guys see all that smoke?"

Standing, Looking, Quiet.

"Come on, something's up."

Go, Go, Stop!

"Yo, one of the towers is on fire!"

Standing, Looking, Quiet.

"Yo, is that a plane?"

Speechless, Breathless, Thoughtless.

"Oh shit!"

Crash!

CHAPTER 6

OVER
&
OVER

To sit in a room,

And be bored out of our minds.

To text away our days and nights.

To go out and have fun.

To laugh so hard,

We lose our breath or begin to cry.

To wrap my arms around you,

And let you know I am there.

To listen to you,

And let you know I care.

To be hurt by you,

Because the pain lets me know,

You are important.

To forgive you,

Because I know that,

You really didn't mean to hurt me.

You can be sure,

I'd relive these experiences over,

And over again.

Because knowing you'd be there with me,

Makes it all worth it.

CHAPTER 7

NEVER OUT

I punched him,

As hard as I could,

Right between his ribs.

Blood in, blood out.

He punched me,

As hard as he could,

Right in my face.

Blood in, blood out.

A mutual hate for,

One another,

Filled our veins,

During that time.

Blood in, blood out.

It was him versus me,

Brother against brother.

Pitted against each,

Other by our,

Very own parents.

Blood in, blood out.

Although the same blood,

Flowed through our veins,

We were divided,

By the circumstances,

Life threw our way.

Blood in, blood out.

Had we completely,

Given in to the malice,

That had been building,

Within us, one of us,

May not be here today.

Blood in, blood out.

Had that been the case,

Then none of us would,

Have made it to today.

Blood in, blood out.

It was during that one,

Day in the park, that,

We realized where we,

Were in life.

We looked back to,

Where we started,

And the fact we were,

Alive was a miracle.

Blood in, blood out.

Though we had fought,

And fought until fatigue,

Had replaced the hate,

Flowing through us,

We had made it to that,

Point in life together.

Blood in, blood out.

We realized that we,

Were just pawns in a,

Game played by the,

Demons that plagued,

Our parents.

Blood in, blood out.

On that day, we truly,

Became brothers.

Not simply because of,

The same blood that,

Flowed within us, but,

Because of the fires,

That molded us and,

The pain that finally,

Bonded us forever.

Blood in, but,

Never out.

CHAPTER 8

LUST
VS
LOVE

Spellbound by one's seduction,

"Hey, wanna make out?"

Befriended by one's kindness,

"Hey, nice to meet you."

Infatuated by one's flesh,

"Damn, she's so fly!"

Blind to one's real beauty,

"Oh hey, what's up?"

Convinced by one's lies,

"I'll call you back, I promise."

Deaf to one's wisdom,

"Wake up Omar, she's a liar!"

Intoxicated by one's kisses,

"This feels so good!"

Unresponsive to one's embrace,

"Just leave me alone."

Hurt by one's neglect,

"I fucking hate that bitch!"

Healed by one's touch,

"I'm so sorry!"

Almost suffocated by lust,

"How could I be so fucking stupid?"

Ultimately saved by true love,

"Don't worry, Omar, I got you."

CHAPTER 9

THE
ENDLESS
CLIMB

<u>Note to Readers:</u>

As might be expected,
The Endless Climb
begins at the bottom.
Please read from bottom to top.

[Just to relive a moment as exhilarating as that one.

[I would climb a thousand flights of stairs,

[We were together, doing what we enjoyed the most.

[Never really caring about reaching the top.

[We climbed, we climbed, and we climbed,

["Hahahaha, you guys are killing me here!"

[We climbed, we climbed, and we climbed.

["Fuck you Vega!"

[We climbed, we climbed, and we climbed.

["But I'm Larino and I'm such a legitimate crybaby, waaaa!"

[We climbed, we climbed, and we climbed.

["Yo, I'm just asking a legitimate question!"

[We climbed, we climbed, and we climbed.

["Waaaa, waaaa! I'm Larino and I'm such a big crybaby!"

[We climbed, we climbed, and we climbed.

["Yo guys, you think we've got much left to go?"

[We climbed, we climbed, and we climbed.

["Hahahahaha!"

[We climbed, we climbed, and we climbed.

["Yo Omar, you're mad stupid bro!"

[We climbed, we climbed, and we climbed.

["Man, both of your moms can catch it!"

[We climbed, we climbed, and we climbed.

["Yeah, well I was with your mom last night, Vega!"

[We climbed, we climbed, and we climbed.

["Yo James, your mom can catch it!"

[We climbed, we climbed, and we climbed.

["God damn it! When will we reach the top?"

[We climbed, we climbed, and we climbed.

71

CHAPTER 10

LATELY

I've been finding myself,

Picturing you in my mind:

Your simple style and nice smile.

I've even been hearing,

Your voice in my head,

At just the mention of your name.

It's become so lovely

And comforting to hear.

What is more,

A pleasant but funny feeling

Engulfs my body,

Whenever I'm in your presence.

I'm beginning to ponder

Why this may be happening?

Because,

When you come around,

I can't help but to,

Smile and become so weightless.

And at night,

I can't help but to,

Just lay in bed and look up,

At the ceiling and wonder all night;

Why I never saw you in this light?

What is this that I am feeling,

That is so unfamiliar to me?

What is this that I am feeling,

That's keeping me up all night?

Why have you been,

Flooding my mind,

Lately?

CHAPTER 11

WE
THREE

In a world of billions,

Yet, we were alone.

In a family of many,

Yet, we were outcasted.

In a circle of friends,

Yet, we were betrayed.

In a brotherhood,

Yet, we were divided.

In a fellowship of truth,

Yet, we were misguided.

In difficult times,

Yet, we persevered.

In paths of our own,

Yet, we remain close.

In ever-changing life,

Yet, we are all we'll ever need.

EPILOGUE

Thankfully, many of the impactful events in my life began when I was very young. Although many of the events that took place early on in my life may be considered to be "harsh" by most, those events laid the groundwork for the foundation I stand on today. During my very first year of college, I was given a series of assignments by my psychology professor, Dr. King. Initially, I did not think much of the assignments as they were just a way to correlate one's life experiences with the psychological behavioral concepts that she was teaching to us in class. However, with each passing assignment, I kept finding myself strolling down memory lane, revisiting what I believe to be the most significant moments of my life.

Whether it was my first or most impactful encounters with domestic violence, love, heartache, or adventure, I was able to recount them all and write them down on paper. What started out as assignments turned into an insightful hobby as the more I wrote, the more I realized about my life and abilities. Admittedly, most of my writings remained stashed away, but then a lovely lady by the name of Carrie Hollister entered my life. If it was not for her, I doubt this book would even exist. Ultimately, it is because of Dr. King and Carrie Hollister that my life was transferred onto paper.

It is my hope that readers of this book gain an understanding of where I started and why the events described in this book are dear to my heart. Even more, I hope that they stay strapped in for the ride that is my life as I have many more writings that detail the years that follow the stories in this book.

To Be Continued

In...

THE PHANTOM
PAIN

Memoirs of a Life Once Hurting

ACKNOWLEDGEMENTS

First and foremost, I would like to thank Dr. Nancy King and Carrie Farrell Hollister. Both of you devoted your time and knowledge to teaching and guiding your students to reach for the absolute pinnacle of their abilities. You did not just do it to see your students have success in your classrooms, but more importantly, you wanted them to succeed in life. My writings would have never come to fruition if it wasn't for what I learned in your classes and I will forever be appreciative of that. I hope that life is treating you both well and that you enjoy reading this book.

I am grateful to Caroline Mackintosh, Masakatsu Watanabe, Todd Moore, and Rick Silvey. Thank you for joining the small group of individuals that have believed in me throughout my life.

Without your guidance, I would not have successfully graduated the University of Saint Mary or been accepted into their Doctorate of Physical Therapy program.

To my mom, my tia Loli, my cousin Delia, and my brothers, Herbert Gonzalez, Joel Vega, James Vazquez, Gregory Brown, and Andrew Torres, I love you all so dearly.

To my lovely wife, Arjelle Lawrence, thank you for loving me and being my rock.

To those of you who have chosen to read this book, thank you!

ABOUT THE AUTHOR

Omar Gonzalez is a former member of the US Armed Forces having been honorably discharged in 2014. He is currently a Doctor of Physical Therapy having graduated from the University of Saint Mary in Leavenworth, KS. More notably, Omar is also the product of a turbulent, alcohol-ridden, and low-income home. He has been  homeless and was not afforded the opportunity of having an all-around safe and fun childhood. However, when speaking to him directly, he would never disclose such information. Instead, Omar would like for people to read about his various experiences in life.

Whether it is encounters with love, heartache, religion, or self-discovery, he has a poem or story for such an experience. When he is not busy with professional endeavors, Omar spends his time thinking of ways to write about his life and does not shy away from using fantastical elements to convey his message. Omar yearns to write emotion-driven stories that captivate the readers' spectrum of emotions and imagination so that they not only feel but also see the story unfold before them. Although writing is not his main pursuit at the moment, it is Omar's hope to have the opportunity to write for many years to come.

WHAT DID YOU THINK?

First of all, thank you for purchasing *The Phantom Struggle*. I know you could have picked any number of books to read, but you picked this book and for that, I am extremely grateful. I hope that it added some value and quality to your everyday life. If so, it would be really nice if you could share this book with your friends and family by posting about it on any social media platforms you may use.

If you enjoyed this book and found some benefit in reading it, I would like to hear from you and hope that you could take some time to post a review on Amazon or wherever you may have purchased the book. I want you to know that your review is very important. Your feedback and support will help me to greatly improve my writing craft for future projects and make this book even better. I wish you all the best in your life and once again, thank you!